THE OFFICIAL
Arsenal
ANNUAL 2018

Written by Josh James
Designed by Jon Dalrymple

A Grange Publication

Manufactured and distributed under licence by Grange Communications Ltd., Edinburgh. Printed in the EU.

Every effort has been made to ensure the accuracy of information within this publication but the publishers cannot be held responsible for any errors or omissions. Views expressed are those of the author and do not necessarily represent those of the publishers or the football club.

Photography © Arsenal Football Club, PA Images and Shutterstock.

ISBN 978 1-911287-64-3

CONTENTS

Dear supporter,

Welcome to the Official Arsenal Annual 2018.

In the end, we made history last season, winning the FA Cup for a record 13th time - but there were lots of highs and lows along the way.

We had a superb performance in the final against Chelsea, and I was very proud of my team for the way they finished the season, after we suffered some damaging defeats in the league.

But our performance at Wembley in the final - and also the semi-final win over Manchester City - showed what this side is capable of, and we aim to produce that level of performance consistently this campaign.

We are in the very unusual position of not being in the Champions League this season, for the first time in nearly 20 years. We are of course upset about that, and as a club we are determined to return there quickly.

I feel we have a squad capable of challenging for all the competitions we are in this season - that is a duty of a big club like ours.

We managed to keep together the vast majority of our squad from last season, and also added two exceptional players in Alexandre Lacazette and Sead Kolasinac. You can read more about both of them in this annual – personally I am convinced they both have what it takes to have a huge impact in the Premier League.

We will need a big contribution from every single member of the squad this season, and you can also read about the rest of our players in these pages, as well as taking part in some quizzes, and looking back on 2016/17.

But for now we are looking forward, and with the support of our fantastic supporters, we know we can achieve more great things together in future. So keep getting right behind the players and club, and enjoy the book!

Arsène Wenger

ROLL OF HONOUR

League champions:
1931, 1933, 1934, 1935, 1938,
1948, 1953, 1971, 1989, 1991,
1998, 2002, 2004

FA Cup winners:
1930, 1936, 1950, 1971, 1979,
1993, 1998, 2002, 2003, 2005,
2014, 2015, 2017

League Cup winners:
1987, 1993

European Fairs Cup winners:
1970

European Cup Winners' Cup winners:
1994

Charity/Community Shield winners:
1930, 1931, 1933, 1934, 1938,
1948, 1953, 1991 (shared), 1998,
1999, 2002, 2004, 2014, 2015, 2017

AUGUST

Our season got off to the worst possible start, with Liverpool coming from behind to claim all three points on the opening day at Emirates Stadium. Theo Walcott netted our first goal of the season but the visitors raced to a 4-1 lead before we struck twice late on. Rob Holding and Granit Xhaka both made their Gunners debuts but it was a day to forget after a promising pre-season. The following weekend we picked up our first point in a goalless draw at the home of champions Leicester, and we got our first win away to Watford seven days later. Three goals came during a very impressive first-half showing, proving more than enough to see off the Hornets. The Gunners were up and running.

AUGUST RESULTS

Sun 14 – Liverpool	H	3-4
Walcott, Oxlade-Chamberlain	Premier League	
Sat 20 – Leicester City	A	0-0
	Premier League	
Sat 27 – Watford	A	3-1
Cazorla, Alexis, Ozil	Premier League	

Arsenal.com August Player of the Month: Laurent Koscielny

SEPTEMBER

Lucas Perez and Shkodran Mustafi arrived before the transfer deadline, and both made their debuts at home to Southampton. A last-gasp penalty from Santi Cazorla, as well as Laurent Koscielny's spectacular equaliser, ensured we took all three points against the Saints. Three days later we travelled to Paris, but our Champions League campaign was barely a minute old before we fell behind to PSG. However, David Ospina made several vital saves, and Alexis grabbed a second-half goal to earn a precious point. Back in England Granit Xhaka scored long-range crackers in each of our next two wins – away to Hull in the Premier League and at Nottingham Forest in the EFL Cup – to set us up nicely for the visit of Chelsea.

SEPTEMBER RESULTS

Sat 10 – Southampton Koscielny, Cazorla	H	2-1	Premier League
Tue 13 – Paris Saint-Germain Alexis	A	1-1	Champions League
Sat 17 – Hull City Alexis 2, Walcott, Xhaka	A	4-1	Premier League
Tue 20 – Nottingham Forest Xhaka, Lucas 2, Oxlade-Chamberlain	A	4-0	EFL Cup
Sat 24 – Chelsea Alexis, Walcott, Ozil	H	3-0	Premier League
Wed 28 – FC Basel Walcott 2	H	2-0	Champions League

SEPTEMBER CONTINUED

Arsène Wenger's men were simply too good for the Blues, running out 3-0 winners with all the goals coming in the opening half. A straightforward home win over Basel in the Champions League – with Theo Walcott bagging a brace – ensured we completed an unbeaten month.

OCTOBER

There was late drama at the start of the month. Laurent Koscielny bundled home an injury-time winner at Burnley, meaning Arsène Wenger could celebrate his 20th anniversary as Arsenal boss with three points. Despite Granit Xhaka's controversial red card at home to Swansea City, we kept up our winning run with a 3-2 victory, and it was seven wins on the spin when we comprehensively saw off Bulgarian side Ludogorets on matchday three of the Champions League group stage. Mesut Ozil was the star that evening, scoring his first professional hat-trick in a 6-0 triumph. Middlesbrough – and their goalkeeper Victor Valdes in particular – were altogether more stubborn opposition however, frustrating the Gunners in a goalless draw. The point was enough to take us top of the league though, and there was more good news as the month drew to a close. Alex Oxlade-Chamberlain scored both goals in the EFL Cup

Arsenal.com October Player of the Month: Mesut Ozil

fourth-round win over Reading and there were also two goals apiece for Alexis Sanchez and Olivier Giroud in a thumping 4-1 win at Sunderland to keep us on top of the Premier League heading into November.

OCTOBER RESULTS

Sun 2 – Burnley		A	1-0
Koscielny		**Premier League**	
Sat 15 – Swansea City		H	3-2
Walcott 2, Ozil		**Premier League**	
Wed 19 – Ludogorets		H	6-0
Alexis, Walcott, Oxlade-Chamberlain, Ozil 3		**Champions League**	
Sat 22 – Middlesbrough		H	0-0
		Premier League	
Tue 25 – Reading		H	2-0
Oxlade-Chamberlain 2		**EFL Cup**	
Sat 29 – Sunderland		A	4-1
Alexis 2, Giroud 2		**Premier League**	

NOVEMBER

A stunning Champions League comeback in Bulgaria kicked off the month. The Gunners were 2-0 down inside 15 minutes against Ludogorets, but Mesut Ozil completed the turnaround with a magnificent solo goal at the death to ensure progression to the last 16 of the competition for the 17th consecutive season. Back on home soil we had to settle for a draw in the north London derby, and Olivier Giroud's late header earned another point at Old Trafford, but it wasn't enough to keep us top of the table. Another draw – this time at home to PSG – also took top spot out of our hands in the Champions League group stage. We returned to winning ways at home to Bournemouth, thanks mainly to an Alexis double, but November ended with defeat in the EFL Cup fifth round at home to Southampton. A much-changed Arsenal side lost 2-0 to the Saints, who ended our 19-game unbeaten run in the process.

NOVEMBER RESULTS

Tue 1 – Ludogorets		A	3-2
Xhaka, Giroud, Ozil		**Champions League**	
Sun 6 – Tottenham		H	1-1
Wimmer (og)		**Premier League**	
Sat 19 – Manchester United		A	1-1
Giroud		**Premier League**	
Wed 23 – Paris Saint-Germain		H	2-2
Giroud, Verratti (og)		**Champions League**	
Sun 27 –Bournemouth		H	3-1
Alexis 2, Walcott		**Premier League**	
Wed 30 –Southampton		H	0-2
		EFL Cup	

Arsenal.com November Player of the Month: Alexis Sanchez

DECEMBER

Alexis Sanchez was the star of the show during our first ever trip to West Ham's new London Stadium. The Chilean scored a hat-trick – the last of which was scored after an outrageous dummy – as we thumped the Hammers 5-1. Three days later Lucas Perez was the hat-trick hero, this time in Switzerland as a convincing 4-1 win was enough to secure top spot from an unbeaten Champions League Group A campaign.

We returned to the summit of the Premier League as well, courtesy of a 3-1 home win over Stoke, when we once again had to come from behind.

But then came successive away defeats that the manager would later describe as the "turning point of the season". First Everton struck late on to win 2-1 at Goodison Park, before Manchester City also came from behind to win by the same scoreline at the Etihad Stadium. Back at Emirates Stadium a late Olivier Giroud header earned a deserved win against West Brom on Boxing Day, and the Gunners were able to end 2016 with three points.

DECEMBER RESULTS

Sat 3 – West Ham United		A	5-1
Ozil, Alexis 3, Oxlade-Chamberlain		Premier League	
Tue 6 – FC Basel		A	4-1
Lucas 3, Iwobi		Champions League	
Sat 10 – Stoke City		H	3-1
Walcott, Ozil, Iwobi		Premier League	
Tue 13 – Everton		A	1-2
Alexis		Premier League	
Sun 18 – Manchester City		A	1-2
Walcott		Premier League	
Mon 26 – West Bromwich Albion		H	1-0
Giroud		Premier League	

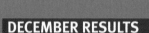

JANUARY

The goals were coming thick and fast as we moved into 2017. And it wasn't just the quantity that was impressive, but the quality as well – especially Olivier Giroud's spectacular 'scorpion kick' at home to Crystal Palace on New Year's Day. The Frenchman's acrobatic, improvised finish laid the foundation for a 2-0 win, and there were more fireworks two days later on the south coast. Bournemouth raced into a shock 3-0 lead but Arsène Wenger's men staged an excellent fightback, eventually taking an unlikely point. A comeback was needed as the FA Cup got under way too. Championship side Preston North End went ahead in the first half, but Giroud was the saviour once again late on to extend the manager's record of never losing at the first hurdle of this competition. A comprehensive win away to Swansea followed, before there was yet more late drama at home to Burnley. The visitors seemed to have snatched a point late on, only for Alexis to coolly chip home a penalty deep in injury-time to grab the win. Danny Welbeck scored twice on his first start of the season, and Theo Walcott netted a hat-trick as we dumped Southampton out of the cup, but there was a shock home reverse to Watford in the Premier League at the end of the month.

JANUARY RESULTS

Sun 1 – Crystal Palace		H	2-0
Giroud, Iwobi			Premier League
Tue 3 – Bournemouth		A	3-3
Alexis, Lucas, Giroud			Premier League
Sat 7 – Preston North End		A	2-1
Ramsey, Giroud			FA Cup
Sat 14 – Swansea City		A	4-0
Giroud, Cork (og), Naughton (og), Alexis			Premier League
Sun 22 – Burnley		H	2-1
Mustafi, Alexis			Premier League
Sat 28 – Southampton		A	5-0
Welbeck 2, Walcott 3			FA Cup
Tue 31 – Watford		H	1-2
Iwobi			Premier League

Arsenal.com January Player of the Month: Olivier Giroud

FEBRUARY

FEBRUARY RESULTS

| Sat 4 – Chelsea | A | 1-3 |
| Giroud | Premier League | |

| Sat 11 – Hull City | H | 2-0 |
| Alexis 2 | Premier League | |

| Wed 15 – Bayern Munich | A | 1-5 |
| Alexis | Champions League | |

| Mon 20 – Sutton United | A | 2-0 |
| Lucas, Walcott | FA Cup | |

Our league title bid finally looked to be buried when Chelsea defeated us 3-1 at Stamford Bridge. Olivier Giroud's late strike proved to be a consolation. Alexis was still in fine goalscoring form though, which he demonstrated with a brace against Hull City at Emirates Stadium. The feel-good factor didn't last long however. The Champions League resumed with a knock-out round tie against familiar foes Bayern Munich in Germany. Alexis netted again to ensure we were level at the break, but after Laurent Koscielny limped off injured, Bayern scored four second-half goals to run out 5-1 winners. So attention switched back to the FA Cup, and an intriguing match against non-league outfit Sutton United. On the artificial surface, the Gunners had too much class for the underdogs, but were made to fight every inch of the way. Lucas opened the scoring in the first half and Theo Walcott sealed our passage through to the quarter-finals with his 100th career goal for the Gunners.

MARCH

Back in the Premier League Liverpool inflicted more misery on us with a 3-1 defeat at Anfield. Danny Welbeck's excellent finish in the second half gave us hope, but a late third killed off our chances and saw us slip below the Reds in the table. Our Champions League exit was confirmed with another damaging defeat to Bayern Munich – another 5-1 reverse, though the scoreline hardly told the story of the game. There was a glimmer of hope we could turn round the first leg deficit when Theo Walcott gave us the lead in a superb first-half performance. But it wasn't to be. Laurent Koscielny was sent off early in the second period and the Germans showed no mercy. We bounced back by beating National League opposition for the second time in a row in the FA Cup. Lincoln City became the first non-league team to reach the quarter-finals for more than 100 years, and held the Gunners until first-half injury time, but were well beaten in the end as Arsène Wenger's men reached a record 29th FA Cup semi-final. However the month ended in more disappointment. We suffered another 3-1 defeat on the road, this time at West Brom, to leave our top four hopes hanging by a thread.

MARCH RESULTS

Sat 4 – Liverpool		A	1-3
Welbeck			Premier League
Tue 7 – Bayern Munich		H	1-5
Walcott			Champions League
Sat 11 – Lincoln City		H	5-0
Walcott, Giroud, Waterfall (og), Alexis, Ramsey			FA Cup
Sat 18 – West Bromwich Albion		A	1-3
Alexis			Premier League

Arsenal.com March Player of the Month: Alexis Sanchez

APRIL

A 2-2 draw at home to Manchester City stopped the rot, and we were back to winning ways with a comfortable win over West Ham at Emirates Stadium. Olivier Giroud's curler was the pick of the goals. The revival was short-lived however. Struggling Crystal Palace ran out 3-0 winners at Selhurst Park in one of the real low points of the season, prompting the manager to switch to a new formation for the next game against Middlesbrough. The back three resulted in three points at the Riverside, and the boss would stick with the new system for the rest of the season. It did the trick at Wembley too. Man City took the lead in the FA Cup semi-final but Nacho Monreal's fine volley took the game to extra-time and Alexis struck the deserved winner to send us back to the final for a record 20th time, and third in the past four years. A late Robert Huth own goal then earned us all three points over Leicester, but Tottenham Hotspur won the last ever north London derby at White Hart Lane to check our progress.

APRIL RESULTS

Sun 2 – Manchester City	H	2-2
Walcott, Mustafi	**Premier League**	
Wed 5 – West Ham United	H	3-0
Ozil, Walcott, Giroud	**Premier League**	
Mon 10 – Crystal Palace	A	0-3
	Premier League	
Mon 17 – Middlesbrough	A	2-1
Alexis, Ozil	**Premier League**	
Sun 23 – Manchester City	N	2-1
Monreal, Alexis	**FA Cup**	
Wed 26 – Leicester City	H	1-0
Huth (og)	**Premier League**	
Sun 30 – Tottenham Hotspur	A	0-2
	Premier League	

Arsenal.com April Player of the Month: Alex Oxlade-Chamberlain

Arsène Wenger secured his first league win over Jose Mourinho when we defeated Manchester United at Emirates Stadium to close the gap on the top four, and three days later we recorded our first victory at St Mary's Stadium since 2003. Alexis opened the scoring on his 100th Premier League outing, making it 20 league goals for the campaign in the process. Another hoodoo was broken in our next game too, away to Stoke. We hadn't won there since 2010, but we turned in a strong, free-flowing performance to blow away the Potters, keeping the pressure on the leading pack. An Alexis brace gave us all three points in an extremely one-sided affair at home to Sunderland, so a top four finish was still a possibility going into the Premier League finale against Everton.

The win was never in doubt from the moment Hector Bellerin gave us an eighth-minute lead, despite Laurent Koscielny seeing red for a reckless challenge and picking up a cup final suspension in the process. But other results didn't go our way, meaning we missed out on Champions League qualification for the first time since 1996/97, even though we surpassed our points tally from last term. The season was not over yet though, next stop Wembley Stadium to meet newly crowned champions Chelsea in the FA Cup final...

MAY RESULTS

Sun 7 – Manchester United	H	2-0	
Xhaka, Welbeck			**Premier League**
Wed 10 – Southampton	A	2-0	
Alexis, Giroud			**Premier League**
Sat 13 – Stoke City	A	4-1	
Giroud 2, Ozil, Alexis			**Premier League**
Tue 16 – Sunderland	H	2-0	
Alexis 2			**Premier League**
Sun 21 – Everton	H	3-1	
Bellerin, Alexis, Ramsey			**Premier League**
Sat 27 – Chelsea	N	2-0	
Alexis, Ramsey			**FA Cup**

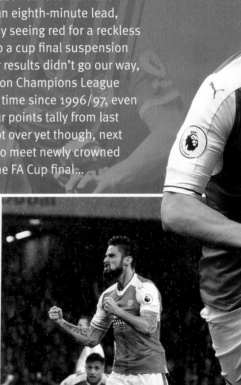

Arsenal.com May Player of the Month: Alexis Sanchez

FA CUP FINAL

Saturday, May 27, 2017

Arsenal 2 (Alexis 5, Ramsey 79) : Chelsea 1 (Costa 76)

Arsenal became the most successful FA Cup side of all time during an unforgettable afternoon at Wembley.

We went into our 20th final in the competition looking for a record 13th win, and the result was scarcely in doubt after a blistering opening five minutes.

We dominated possession in the early exchanges, and were rewarded when Alexis burst through and tucked the ball home. Chelsea were appealing for offside, but Aaron Ramsey wasn't interfering with play and the goal stood.

Mesut Ozil then had an effort cleared off the line before we went even closer – Danny Welbeck striking the post.

In the second half Victor Moses was sent off for a second bookable offence, but 10-man Chelsea immediately hit back. Diego Costa finished well with their first real effort of the match.

Team: Ospina, Mertesacker, Holding, Monreal, Oxlade-Chamberlain (Coquelin 82), Xhaka, Bellerin, Ramsey, Alexis (Elneny 90), Ozil, Welbeck (Giroud 78).

"It's been an up-and-down season, but to finish it with an FA Cup has to make it a successful one. I just love this competition. The boys deserve it, and I'm happy for the manger, I'm delighted. He's been fantastic for me, fantastic for these players. Fair play to him, he's changed the system and it's paid off."

Aaron Ramsey

FA CUP WINNERS!

It was our turn to respond, and we did so in style. Substitute Olivier Giroud sent in a dangerous cross with virtually his first touch, and there was Ramsey to prod home the winner. It was the second time the Welshman had claimed the clinching goal in an FA Cup final, following his heroics against Hull City in 2014.

David Ospina made a fine save near the death as we held on to seal the club's 44th major honour overall, and third FA Cup in the past four seasons. For Arsène Wenger it was his seventh success in the competition, making him the most decorated manager in FA Cup history, breaking a 97-year record.

Most successful teams in FA Cup history

Club	Wins
Arsenal	13
Manchester United	12
Tottenham Hotspur	8
Liverpool	7
Chelsea	7
Aston Villa	7
Newcastle United	6
Blackburn Rovers	6
Everton	5
West Bromwich Albion	5
Manchester City	5
Wanderers	5

We asked our players to cast their minds back to their childhood, and remember what life was like when they were 10 years old.

My biggest fear...

Olivier Giroud: This is so funny, but my brothers are older than me – I was the youngest, and they used to tease me about a cartoon figure called Alf. Do you know him? Alf the Alien, my god he was so ugly and I was so scared of him. My brothers used to say to me 'Be careful, Alf is going to get you tonight!' They went too far with it!

Nacho Monreal: Spiders and snakes. I hate them!

Mesut Ozil: I was actually really scared of dogs at that time! It was only when I got my own one that I had to overcome my fear. Now I love them.

Petr Cech: I badly broke my leg when I was 10, and my biggest fear was that my leg wouldn't be all right after the injury and I would miss out on all the things I liked doing.

My pets were...

Rob Holding: A rabbit and a hamster, the rabbit was called Todd and my hamster was called Kevin, my sister's was Elvis.

Petr Cech: I had a hamster, a guinea pig and then later my older sister got a sausage dog.

My nickname was...

Francis Coquelin: Everybody used to call me Cisco. Somebody called me Francisco and then that got shortened to Cisco. I never get called it here at Arsenal, but whenever I see my friends from home they still call me that. It's stuck.

Per Mertesacker: I got called 'langer' because I was already quite tall and long. Langer means long one.

Olivier Giroud: I had plenty of nicknames! My brothers used to give them to me, but I don't want to tell you any of those. People used to call me Olive.

Nacho Monreal: They called me Cabra. It means goat, but don't ask me why!

The silliest thing I did was...

David Ospina: I once jumped off the highest step of a flight of stairs!

Granit Xhaka: I was quite sensible really. I never did anything like skip school or steal or mess around that much, I might have smashed a window playing football though.

Mesut Ozil: Mess around now and again. I was once stupid with fireworks but I'm not telling you what I got up to!

My favourite footballer was...

Olivier Giroud: Probably Zidane at around that age, especially when we won the World Cup a couple of years later. Then after that it was always Andrey Shevchenko.

Granit Xhaka: Zinedine Zidane, but I have nice memories of watching players like the Yakin brothers, Christian Gimenez and Matias Delgado at Basel. I still remember Benjamin Huggel and Marco Streller too.

Laurent Koscielny: Probably Chris Waddle, when he played for Marseille. He was part of a very special team and I also liked the other top players like Jean-Pierre Papin, Abedi Pele and Basile Boli. I liked that whole generation.

Mohamed Elneny: My favourite player was Thierry Henry.

My bedtime was...

Emi Martinez: Very late! My brother was older than me so we used to play on the PlayStation until about 2am sometimes!

Rob Holding: My dad would like to think it was 10pm but I was always up on the Xbox until God knows what time in the morning!

Hector Bellerin: Always around 11 or 11.30pm. In Spain we used to have dinner quite late, especially when we were training. Sometimes I'd get home about 11pm, have dinner and go straight to bed.

I hoped dinner would be....

Olivier Giroud: Well I come from the Alps so I liked melted cheese, raclette. It's amazing.

Emi Martinez: Asada. It's a typical Argentinian barbecue meat dish.

Nacho Monreal: Just a salad with eggs, or a sandwich.

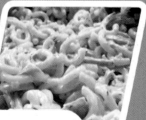

Francis Coquelin: Pasta, and that's still the case now. I love pasta!

My worst habit was...

Petr Cech: breaking tennis rackets! I have always taken things seriously, and when I was losing I wasn't angry towards my opponent, but angry towards myself. I had to let that steam off somehow, and usually I took it out on my racket! I think I broke two rackets. My other bad habit was that I could never sit still!

Francis Coquelin: Eating too much food. I ate so much sugar when I was 10.

The other sports I loved were....

Alexis Sanchez: I liked basketball and tennis and used to play them a lot. My brother and I played tennis – he always won!

Per Mertesacker: I used to love roller skating. I was very proud of my roller skates.

David Ospina: Basketball and volleyball.

Mesut Ozil: I loved sport, I like basketball, go-karting and I played table tennis too. I was really good at that actually.

Rob Holding: Cricket. I was a bowler, I wasn't a batsman at all! I don't play anymore, I don't have the time or the right place to play but I wouldn't mind playing a little bit. I did a bit of rugby sevens too but wasn't allowed to play full-on rugby.

Arsenal meant....

Mohamed Elneny: They were the team I supported in Europe and Al Ahly was my team in Egypt as I was playing for them. I loved Arsenal because of players such as Henry, Pires, Ljungberg, and because of their style as a team.

Hector Bellerin: There are a lot of people who might not believe it, but I used to have a Thierry Henry Arsenal shirt that my mum bought me. I still have it back in Spain actually.

Granit Xhaka: A team that played attractive football. I used to enjoy watching Arsenal when I was younger. In fact, I'd watch a lot of Premier League games. I remember the likes of Thierry Henry, Patrick Vieira and Robert Pires really well.

Francis Coquelin: Would you believe that when I was 10, for Christmas I got my first football shirt and it was an Arsenal shirt, with my name on the back. It's true, it was meant to be.

We asked some of our first-team stars for their autograph, and got them to explain the story behind their signatures...

Olivier Giroud

When did you first practice your autograph?

Maybe it was on my identity card, when I was about 10 or 11 years old, that's when I first tried it.

Can you remember the very first time you signed for a fan?

Not exactly. It was maybe when I was at Grenoble, when I started my career. I have a feeling the first one was on a shirt. I guess I was about 19 or 20, but I can tell you straightaway that I wasn't asked very often back then!

Did you get many autographs when you were a kid?

Not really because I basically didn't see many celebrities or footballers. I met Zidane one time when he was in my town, I was about 10, and that was very exciting, but I didn't manage to get his autograph – it was too busy!

Rob Holding

Has your autograph always looked like this?

Yeah, pretty much. It's always just had the R for Robert and then just my second name basically. I know some people have something that looks nothing like their name, but I've always liked to have it so you can read R Holding, rather than it just being a scribble.

When was the first time you were asked for an autograph?

I can remember it, I was at Bolton, and had played a few games. I was coming out of the stadium one day, kids were waiting there and they said 'Rob, can you sign my programme for me.' That was the first time I remember signing something.

As a kid who did you ask for an autograph?

No-one really, we were always playing youth games when the first-team were playing, then before I knew it I was in the team too, so I couldn't ask for theirs! I never really had an autograph book or anything, but when we went to Florida when I was five or six, we went round seeing all the characters at Disneyland, so I had a picture with Mickey Mouse and everyone. That's probably the only time I have got autographs.

Alex Iwobi

Has your autograph always looked like this?

Sort of, it's evolved over time. It used to be easy to write because I was lazy and just put my first initial followed by my surname, but then my dad told me I needed to make it more difficult for people to forge. Now I just scribble a lot!

Can you remember when you first practiced your autograph?

I was in school and I definitely regret doing this, but I used to practice my signature by writing on the tables. Thank goodness my teacher didn't notice me doing that!

What's the most unusual place you've been asked to sign... and did you sign it?

On my last holiday I was near a swimming pool and a guy asked me to sign his belly. I remember thinking, 'I'm not going to sign your belly if it's just going to wash off in the pool'. That's definitely the strangest place, especially as it was at a swimming pool as well.

Granit Xhaka

Has your autograph always looked like this?

No, in my first year as a professional it was a different autograph, but for the past three or four years it's been the same. I won't change it again now, it's my signature and I'm happy with it.

When was the first time you were asked for an autograph?

I think it was probably my brother, Taulant. I took his shirt, he took mine and we asked for each other's signature on them. I think that must have been the first time I ever signed my shirt or anything.

As a kid can you ever remember asking someone for an autograph, apart from your brother?

Yes, Roger Federer, the tennis player. He is a legend in Switzerland and all over the world. I have his signature because he came to FC Basel when I was about 18 or 19. He is a Basel fan, so he used to come to the games, and the first time I met him I got his signature, and I still have it at home.

Danny Welbeck

Can you remember when you first practiced your autograph?

I think it was when I was back in my youth team days. When you first get asked for one, you realise you need to practice!

How many autographs do you think you sign each day on average now?

It depends what I do. Most days I just train and go home anyway, so I don't see many people, but if I'm out in town I will sign quite a few, maybe 10 a week. Whenever I go into central London I'm prepared to sign quite a few!

As a kid can you ever remember asking someone for an autograph – who?

I wasn't really an autograph hunter. It was only sometimes that I came across first team players when I was at United that I got the chance. I did get David Beckham's signature though.

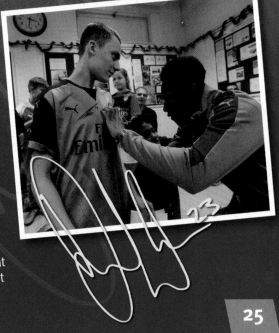

HEAD TO HEAD

We are currently playing our 26th Premier League season – we are one of six ever-present teams in the competition. Here is our all-time record against the other 19 teams, as at the start of this season.

KEY

Opposition Team

Games played | Games won | Games drawn | Games lost

Goals scored | Goals conceded

Bournemouth

4 3 1 0

10 4

Brighton & Hove Albion

Never met in Premier League

Burnley

6 5 1 0

11 3

Chelsea

50 19 14 17

64 68

Crystal Palace

16 11 3 2

29 12

Everton

50 30 13 7

95 43

Huddersfield Town

Never met in Premier League

Leicester City

22 14 7 1

49 18

Liverpool

50 15 17 18

63 74

Manchester City

⚽	😊	😐	☹️
40	23	10	7

👍 68 👎 38

Manchester United

⚽	😊	😐	☹️
50	13	15	22

👍 51 👎 70

Newcastle United
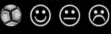

⚽	😊	😐	☹️
44	25	10	9

👍 72 👎 38

Southampton

⚽	😊	😐	☹️
36	20	10	6

👍 66 👎 35

Stoke City

⚽	😊	😐	☹️
18	11	3	4

👍 34 👎 16

Swansea City

⚽	😊	😐	☹️
12	6	1	5

👍 21 👎 15

Tottenham Hotspur

⚽	😊	😐	☹️
50	18	21	11

👍 80 👎 61

Watford

⚽	😊	😐	☹️
8	7	0	1

👍 20 👎 6

West Bromwich Albion

⚽	😊	😐	☹️
22	15	3	4

👍 44 👎 23

West Ham United

⚽	😊	😐	☹️
42	27	8	7

👍 78 👎 30

Our overall Premier League record

⚽	😊	😐	☹️
962	525	247	190

👍 1,698 👎 911

Can you find the eight differences between these two pictures?

Solutions on page 61.

Arsenal have won the FA Cup a record 13 times, so here are 13 questions on the oldest knockout competition in world football.

1. Which player set up Aaron Ramsey's goals in both the 2014 and 2017 finals?

2. How many times has Arsène Wenger won the FA Cup for Arsenal?

3. Which colour kit did Arsenal wear when we won the 2015 final?

4. Which team did Arsenal beat on penalties in the 2005 final?

5. In which year did we first win the FA Cup? 1910, 1920 or 1930?

6. Which of the following players played in five FA Cup finals for Arsenal: David Seaman, Patrick Vieira or Dennis Bergkamp?

7. True or false, the 2003 FA Cup final was the only final to be played under a roof?

8. How many goals were scored in the last five minutes of the 1979 FA Cup final against Manchester United?

9. What was the score at half-time of the 2014 FA Cup final against Hull City?

10. What did Arsenal need in the 1993 final that we have not needed in any other final?

11. Name one of the two scorers in the 2002 final against Chelsea.

12. In which season did we beat Newcastle United 2-0 in the final?

13. Arsenal recorded the biggest winning scoreline in an FA Cup final for 20 years when we beat Aston Villa in 2015. What was the score?

Solutions on page 61.

Recognise this lot?!

We think you'll agree they all look better in the red and white of Arsenal, but this was how they looked right at the start of their careers. Let's take a walk down memory lane...

Our goalkeeper had just turned 19 when this photo was taken in July 2001. He was at Sparta Prague in his home country at the time, he stayed there for just one season before moving to Rennes in France, he then came to the Premier League in 2004.

PETR CECH

This photo was taken ahead of Spain's match against England at the European Under-21 Championship in June 2009. Monreal was an Osasuna player at the time, and a couple of months later he became a senior international. In 2011 he joined Malaga, where he spent a year and a half before becoming a Gunner.

NACHO MONREAL

Cazorla was 20 years old when this photo was taken, in February 2005. The midfielder is seen celebrating a goal for Villarreal in the UEFA Cup – he made more than 200 appearances for the club in two spells before he joined Monreal at Malaga. Cazorla had just one season there, then left Spain for Arsenal in 2012.

SANTI CAZORLA

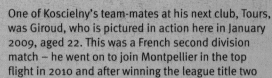

You will probably recognise both players in this picture. Koscielny was 19 here, playing for Guingamp against Emmanuel Adebayor's Monaco in the French League in December 2004. Guingamp was Koscielny's first senior club. He soon moved onto Tours, then Lorient before moving across the Channel in 2010.

One of Koscielny's team-mates at his next club, Tours, was Giroud, who is pictured in action here in January 2009, aged 22. This was a French second division match – he went on to join Montpellier in the top flight in 2010 and after winning the league title two seasons later, he made his way to north London.

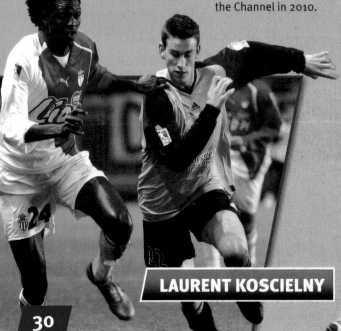

LAURENT KOSCIELNY

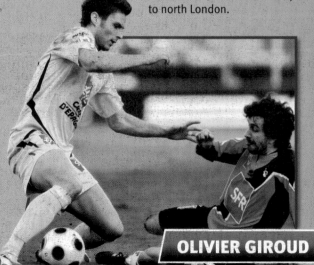

OLIVIER GIROUD

It's photocall time for Schalke in July 2006, and Ozil lines up for his first season as a senior pro. The German was 17 in this photo, and just 18 months later he moved to Werder Bremen. Real Madrid was his next port of call in 2010, and he became Arsenal's record signing when he transferred from the Spanish capital in 2013.

MESUT OZIL

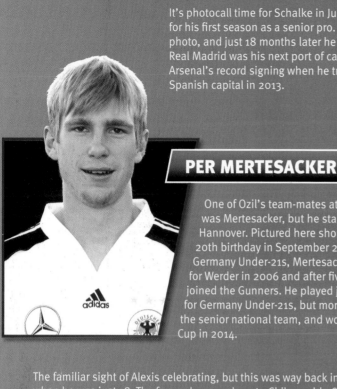

PER MERTESACKER

One of Ozil's team-mates at Werder Bremen was Mertesacker, but he started out at Hannover. Pictured here shortly before his 20th birthday in September 2004, lining up for Germany Under-21s, Mertesacker left Hannover for Werder in 2006 and after five years there he joined the Gunners. He played just three times for Germany Under-21s, but more than 100 for the senior national team, and won the World Cup in 2014.

The familiar sight of Alexis celebrating, but this was way back in March 2007, when he was just 18. The forward was on loan to Chilean side Colo Colo at the time, playing in South America's equivalent of the Champions League, the Copa Libertadores. He was loaned to Colo Colo by Udinese, who sold him to Barcelona in 2011. After three seasons in Spain, and one league title, he joined Arsenal in 2014.

ALEXIS SANCHEZ

AARON RAMSEY

This photo was taken at Emirates Stadium, but Ramsey had no idea he would later call the place home when he was in action for Cardiff Under-18s in the FA Youth Cup way back in February 2007. The midfielder was just 16 at the time, and the young Gunners – including Kieran Gibbs – were too good for Ramsey's side on the day. A little over a year later Ramsey and Gibbs were team-mates in the Arsenal first team.

Also in action in the FA Youth Cup at Emirates Stadium that season was Welbeck, playing for Manchester United Under-18s. Welbeck was just 16 at the time, and he helped his side eliminate Arsenal to reach the final. Seven years later he returned to Emirates Stadium, to sign for the Gunners.

DANNY WELBECK

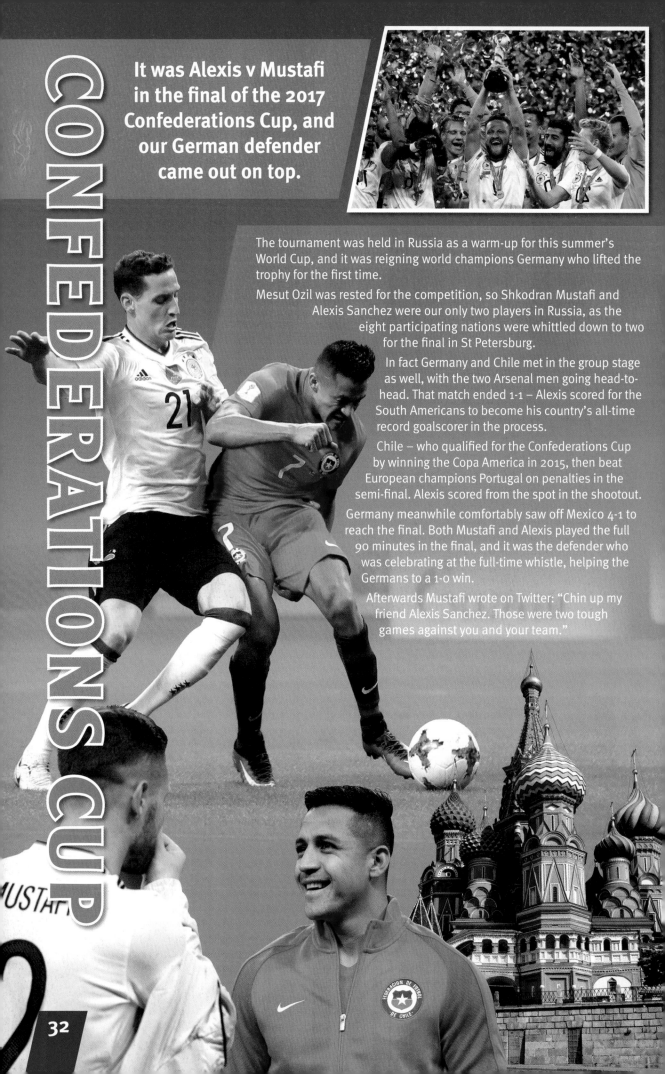

It was Alexis v Mustafi in the final of the 2017 Confederations Cup, and our German defender came out on top.

The tournament was held in Russia as a warm-up for this summer's World Cup, and it was reigning world champions Germany who lifted the trophy for the first time.

Mesut Ozil was rested for the competition, so Shkodran Mustafi and Alexis Sanchez were our only two players in Russia, as the eight participating nations were whittled down to two for the final in St Petersburg.

In fact Germany and Chile met in the group stage as well, with the two Arsenal men going head-to-head. That match ended 1-1 – Alexis scored for the South Americans to become his country's all-time record goalscorer in the process.

Chile – who qualified for the Confederations Cup by winning the Copa America in 2015, then beat European champions Portugal on penalties in the semi-final. Alexis scored from the spot in the shootout.

Germany meanwhile comfortably saw off Mexico 4-1 to reach the final. Both Mustafi and Alexis played the full 90 minutes in the final, and it was the defender who was celebrating at the full-time whistle, helping the Germans to a 1-0 win.

Afterwards Mustafi wrote on Twitter: "Chin up my friend Alexis Sanchez. Those were two tough games against you and your team."

QUIZ WHO'S OLDER?

Here are ten pairs of Gunners, past and present.
Just tell us, out of each pair, which player is older.

1. Alexandre Lacazette or Mesut Ozil?

2. Per Mertesacker or Laurent Koscielny?

3. Aaron Ramsey or Sead Kolasinac?

4. Hector Bellerin or Rob Holding?

5. Granit Xhaka or Mohamed Elneny?

6. Danny Welbeck or Theo Walcott?

7. Sol Campbell or Kolo Toure?

8. Patrick Vieira or Ray Parlour?

9. Ian Wright or Dennis Bergkamp?

10. Robert Pires or Thierry Henry?

The Gunners scored 121 goals last season, including some absolute crackers. It's the most goals we have scored in a season for more than 80 years. But which was your favourite? Here's a reminder of some of the best.

Koscielny's bicycle kick

Arsenal 2, Southampton 1 – September 10, 2016
Laurent Koscielny celebrated his birthday in fine style, scoring a spectacular overhead kick to equalise against Southampton in our first home game of the season. It's not often you see a goal of such quality, but it's even rarer to see a centre half pull off such a stunning piece of skill.

Xhaka's screamer

Hull City 1, Arsenal 4 – September 17, 2016
What a way to open your account for the club. Swiss midfielder Granit Xhaka was making only his fifth appearance since joining in the summer, and unleashed a 30-yard rocket with his left boot into the top corner to cap an excellent away win. And to prove it was no fluke, three days later he scored a near identical goal away to Nottingham Forest in the EFL Cup.

Walcott's team goal

Arsenal 3, Chelsea 0 – September 24, 2016
The Gunners ripped into Chelsea in the first half at Emirates Stadium, and this was the pick of the three goals we scored before the break. Theo Walcott, Santi Cazorla, Mesut Ozil and Alex Iwobi all swapped quick passes as we broke into the area at pace, before Hector Bellerin squared from the right to give the England man a tap in. Emirates Stadium erupted.

Ozil's dummy

Ludogorets 2, Arsenal 3 – November 1, 2016
Things were looking bleak when we found ourselves 2-0 down in Bulgaria, but there was to be a sting in the tail, and what a sting. Having fought back to level, Mohamed Elneny then found Mesut Ozil with a long pass late on. The German perfectly lofted the ball over the advancing keeper, kept his composure in the box to send two defenders flying with a delicious dummy before rolling home the winner.

Alexis's stepover

West Ham 1, Arsenal 5 – December 3, 2016
Arsenal's first ever trip to West Ham's London Stadium will always be remembered for a superb Alexis hat-trick, and his last was the best of the lot. Racing clear of the offside trap late on, he found himself one-on-one with Darren Randolph in the West Ham goal. He completely wrong-footed the keeper with a cheeky stepover, then casually clipped the ball into the net.

5

Giroud's scorpion

Arsenal 2, Crystal Palace 0 – January 1, 2017
A goal that had all the football world talking. Launching a counter-attack from his own half, Olivier Giroud sprinted forward to get on the end of Alexis's cross. The Frenchman then, somehow, contrived to volley in by extending his leg up and behind him and flicking the ball with pace, off the outside of his foot, in off the bar from 11 yards out. It was a goal of such stunning execution that it left the Emirates crowd gasping in awe, and those watching on television eager for more replays to see exactly how he had managed it.

6

Lucas's volley

Bournemouth 3, Arsenal 3 – January 3, 2017
From the tightest of angles, Lucas Perez smashed home a left-foot volley to help Arsenal come back from 3-0 down at Bournemouth, and ultimately earn a point. With 15 minutes remaining, and the score at 3-1, Giroud flicked the ball up over Lucas's head, and the Spaniard watched it all the way onto his left foot before flashing a shot past the keeper and just inside the far post.

7

Ramsey's curler

Arsenal 3, Everton 1 – May 21, 2017
Our last goal of the Premier League season was also one of the best. In the last minute of the match Ozil tricked his way past Mason Holgate, then teed up Aaron Ramsey on the edge of the area. The Welshman turned, took aim then bent a delicious shot into the top corner, past the despairing keeper. Ramsey had found his shooting boots, just in time for the following week's FA Cup final...

8

THE GOALSCORERS

Player	Goals
Alexis Sanchez	30
Theo Walcott	19
Olivier Giroud	16
Mesut Ozil	12
Lucas Perez	7
Alex Oxlade-Chamberlain	6
Alex Iwobi	4
Granit Xhaka	4
Danny Welbeck	4
Aaron Ramsey	4
Santi Cazorla	2
Laurent Koscielny	2
Shkodran Mustafi	2
Hector Bellerin	1

List your top 3   **1** ?   **2** ?   **3** ?

New name, new faces, new season!

It's all change at Arsenal Women FC for 2017/18. The first change is the name – no longer is the team known as Arsenal Ladies, but Arsenal Women.

The second change is to the schedule. After six years of playing throughout the summer months, women's football in England returned to a winter calendar this season.

To get the teams geared up for the new campaign, a shorter Spring Series was staged, between nine of the sides that make up this season's FA Women's Super League 1. The Gunners finished the Spring Series unbeaten, with five wins and three draws from their eight games, but that was only enough for a third-place finish, one point behind Manchester City and champions Chelsea.

But the biggest change is to the playing staff at Arsenal. The Spring Series allowed Pedro Martinez's team to gel and prepare for this season, with plenty of new faces added to the squad over the past year.

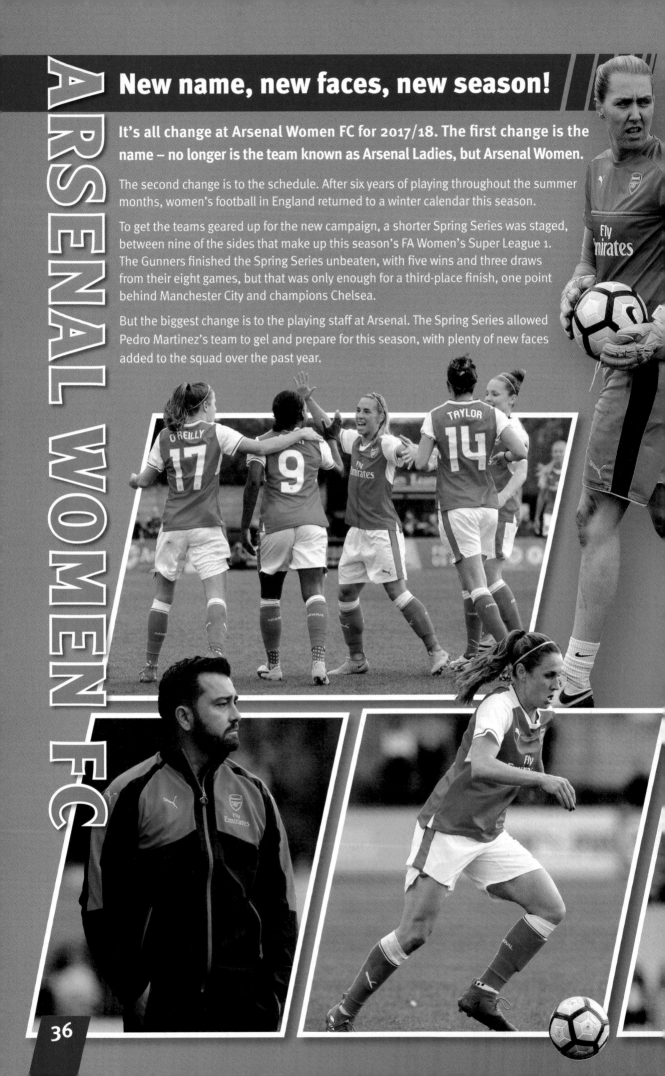

Here's your guide to the new players in this season.

Heather O'Reilly

Position: Midfielder

A hugely experienced USA international midfielder, World Cup winner and three-time Olympic champion, who joined in January 2017.

Louise Quinn

Position: Defender

Established Ireland international central defender who joined from Notts County in May 2017, on a short-term deal.

Kim Little

Position: Midfielder

Scotland international who returned to Arsenal in January 2017, from Seattle Reign, having scored 81 times in her first Gunners spell.

Vivianne Miedema

Position: Forward

Prolific Dutch forward who signed from Bayern Munich in May 2017, then won the European Championships shortly afterwards.

Beth Mead

Position: Forward

Signed in January 2017, at the age of 21, from Sunderland, where she scored 77 times in 78 games.

Lisa Evans

Position: Midfielder

Scotland international winger who signed from Bayern Munich in June 2017, aged 25.

Anna Moorhouse

Position: Goalkeeper

Young back up goalkeeper who signed from Doncaster Belles ahead of the Spring Series in February 2017.

Jessica Samuelsson

Position: Defender

Experienced right back who won a silver medal at the 2016 Olympic Games with Sweden. Signed from Linkopings in August 2017.

Josephine Henning

Position: Defender

Germany international central defender Josy re-signed for the Gunners after one season at Lyon, where she won the treble to add to her impressive tally of honours.

13 DAVID OSPINA

Colombia international keeper David finished last season in the best possible fashion – starring in the FA Cup final victory over Chelsea. The athletic shot-stopper kept four clean sheets in 14 appearances – mainly featuring in European competition – and is now in his fourth season at the club. The most capped goalkeeper in his country's history, he joined the Gunners from French side Nice, after starring at the 2014 World Cup.

EMILIANO MARTINEZ 26

Having joined Arsenal as a teenager back in 2010, Emi is now in his eighth season at the club, where he continues to make excellent progress. He made five more first-team appearances last term, keeping three clean sheets, in the Premier League and League Cup. Truly a goalkeeper in the modern mold with good distribution and excellent reflexes, the former Argentine youth international has had four loan spells at English clubs, and this season is on loan at Spanish side Getafe.

33 PETR CECH

One of the most successful goalkeepers in European football, Petr proved his worth to the club again last season, with a string of excellent performances. He missed just three league games during 2016/17, and kept 12 clean sheets. The most capped Czech Republic international of all time, he was named Czech Player of the Season for an incredible 11th time last term. He joined us from Chelsea in 2015, where he won nine major honours, including the Champions League.

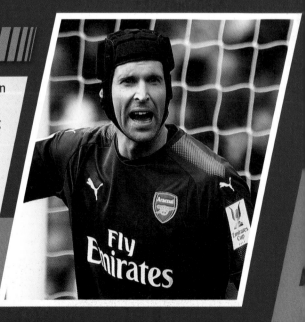

PLAYER PROFILES

DEFENDERS

2 MATHIEU DEBUCHY

Combative right back Mathieu is entering his fourth year with us, having joined from Newcastle United in the summer of 2014. The France international defender, who featured at Euro 2012 and the 2014 World Cup, has been unlucky with injuries during most of his Gunners career, and played just once last season – starting the 3-1 win over Bournemouth. Before coming to England Mathieu was a league title winner during a ten-year stint at Lille.

PER MERTESACKER 4

Club captain Per was restricted to just one start last season due to injury – but what a time to make it. The towering German central defender turned in a faultless performance in the FA Cup final, before getting his hands on the trophy for the third time. A natural leader both on the pitch and in the dressing room, Per was a World Cup winner in 2014, but has since retired from international football with more than 100 caps to his name.

Player	Born	Joined Arsenal	Previous Clubs	Arsenal Debut
David Ospina	Medellin, Colombia, Aug 31, 1988	from Nice on July 27, 2014	Atletico Nacional, Nice	v Southampton (h) League Cup, Sept 23, 2014
Emiliano Martinez	Buenos Aires, Argentina, Sept 2, 1992	from Independiente on Aug 1, 2010	Independiente, Oxford Utd (loan), Sheff Wed (loan), Rotherham Utd (loan), Wolves (loan)	v Coventry City (H), League Cup, Sept 26, 2012
Petr Cech	Pilsen, Czech Republic, May 20, 1982	from Chelsea on June 29, 2015	Chmel Blsany, Sparta Prague, Rennes, Chelsea	v Chelsea (n) Community Shield, Aug 2, 2015
Mathieu Debuchy	Fretin, France, July 28, 1985	from Newcastle United on July 17, 2014	Lille, Newcastle United, Bordeaux (loan)	v Man City (n) Community Shield, Aug 10, 2014
Per Mertesacker	Hannover, Germany, Sept 29, 1984	from Werder Bremen on Aug 31, 2011	Hannover 96, Werder Bremen	v Swansea City (h) League, Sept 10, 2011

6 LAURENT KOSCIELNY

Widely regarded as one of the best central defenders in Europe, Laurent has been a key member of the Arsenal team since 2010, when he arrived from French side Lorient. Usually captaining the side in Per Mertesacker's absence last season, Laurent is a controlling, composed presence in the centre of our defence, and often contributes vital goals as well. A valuable member of the France squad, he has featured at each of the last three major international tournaments.

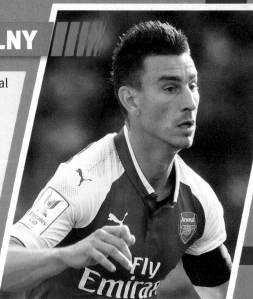

ROB HOLDING 16

Young defender Rob had a debut season to remember, following his transfer from Championship side Bolton Wanderers. After appearing in the first few games of the season, he won back his place in time to star at Wembley in both the FA Cup semi-final and final. A ball-playing centre back who is calm in possession, England Under-21 international Rob made a big impression last term, continuing his rapid progression since making his senior debut, aged 19, in 2015.

18 NACHO MONREAL

A steady and unflappable presence in the Arsenal defence, Nacho showed his versatility last season, appearing very much at home either at left back or more centrally as part of a back three. He missed just two league games in 2016/17, and netted his only goal of the campaign to win the FA Cup semi-final at Wembley. A full Spain international since 2009, Nacho has been Mr Consistent for the Gunners following his transfer from Malaga midway through the 2012/13 season.

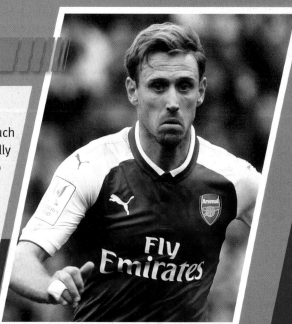

20 SHKODRAN MUSTAFI

A high-profile signing from Valencia just before the summer transfer deadline, Shkodran remained unbeaten for the first 22 games of his Gunners career. The talented central defender scored his first goal for us during that sequence – a header in the home win over Burnley. He later netted against Manchester City and played 37 times in all during his first season here. A World Cup winner with Germany in 2014, Shkodran was part of Everton's youth setup under David Moyes, then had successful spells in Italy with Sampdoria and in Spain with Valencia before becoming a Gunner.

CALUM CHAMBERS 21

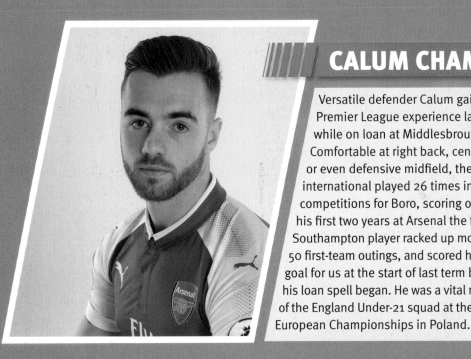

Versatile defender Calum gained more Premier League experience last season while on loan at Middlesbrough. Comfortable at right back, centre back or even defensive midfield, the England international played 26 times in all competitions for Boro, scoring once. In his first two years at Arsenal the former Southampton player racked up more than 50 first-team outings, and scored his third goal for us at the start of last term before his loan spell began. He was a vital member of the England Under-21 squad at the 2017 European Championships in Poland.

Player	Born	Joined Arsenal	Previous Clubs	Arsenal Debut
Laurent Koscielny	Tulle, France, Sept 10, 1985	from Lorient on July 2, 2010	Guingamp, Tours, Lorient	v Liverpool (a) League, Aug 15, 2010
Rob Holding	Tameside, Sept 20, 1995	from Bolton Wanderers on July 22, 2016	Bolton Wanderers, Bury (loan)	v Liverpool (h) League, Aug 14, 2016
Nacho Monreal	Pamplona, Spain, Feb 26, 1986	from Malaga on Jan 31, 2013	Osasuna, Malaga	v Stoke City (h) League, Feb 2, 2013
Shkodran Mustafi	Bad Hersfeld, Germany, Apr 17, 1992	from Valencia on Aug 29, 2016	Everton, Sampdoria, Valencia	v Southampton (h) League, Sept 10, 2016
Calum Chambers	Petersfield, Jan 20, 1995	from Southampton on July 28, 2014	Southampton, Middlesbrough (loan)	v Man City (n) Community Shield, Aug 10, 2014

24 HECTOR BELLERIN

Speedy right back Hector has quickly established himself as one of the best attacking full backs on the continent. The Spain international made his debut for us in 2013 at the age of 18, and hasn't looked back since, making more than 100 first-team appearances to date. He ended last season by lifting his second FA Cup with us, after a fine showing in the final at Wembley. Moving to the Arsenal Academy from Barcelona aged 16, Hector signed a new long-term contract with us in November 2016.

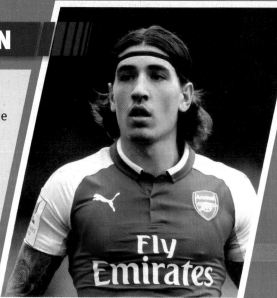

MIDFIELDERS

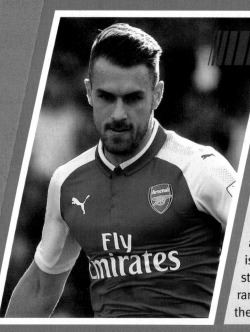

AARON RAMSEY 8

For the second time in four years, Aaron scored the winning goal for us in the FA Cup final, when he headed home in the second half against Chelsea at Wembley. It was the indefatigable midfielder's fourth goal of the campaign, and came a week after his stunning strike against Everton. Now in his 10th season with us after joining from hometown club Cardiff at the age of 17, Wales international Aaron is a box-to-box midfielder with fantastic stamina levels, and an impressive passing range. He was named in the UEFA Team of the Tournament at Euro 2016.

Player	Born	Joined Arsenal	Previous Clubs	Arsenal Debut
Hector Bellerin	Barcelona, Spain, Mar 19, 1995	as a scholar in summer 2011	Watford (loan)	v West Brom (a), League Cup, Sept 25, 2013
Aaron Ramsey	Caerphilly, Wales, Dec 26, 1990	from Cardiff City on June 13, 2008	Cardiff City, Nottingham Forest (loan), Cardiff City (loan)	v FC Twente (a) Champions League, Aug 13, 2008
Jack Wilshere	Hertfordshire, Jan 1, 1992	as a scholar in summer 2008	Bolton Wanderers (loan), Bournemouth (loan)	v Blackburn Rovers (a) League, Sept 13, 2008
Mesut Ozil	Gelsenkirchen, Germany, Oct 15, 1988	from Real Madrid on Sept 2, 2013	Schalke, Werder Bremen, Real Madrid	v Sunderland (a) League, Sept 14, 2013
Santi Cazorla	Llanera, Spain, Dec 13, 1984	from Malaga on Aug 7, 2012	Villarreal, Villarreal B, Recreativo Huelva, Malaga	v Sunderland (h) League, Aug 18, 2012

10 JACK WILSHERE

Last season Jack impressed while on loan at Bournemouth, as he returned to full fitness following a frustrating period out with injury. The stylish, competitive midfielder, who joined the Arsenal Academy at the age of nine, was named PFA Young Player of the Year in 2010/11 shortly after making his senior international debut for England. Comfortable in either a defensive or more creative midfield role, Jack scored BBC Match of the Day's Goal of the Season in both 2013/14 and 2014/15.

MESUT OZIL 11

A supremely gifted playmaker, Mesut is the creative spark behind so many of our attacking moves. The Germany international, who won the World Cup in 2014, reached double figures for both goals and assists last season. One of the highlights of his campaign was a wonderful hat-trick at home to Ludogorets in the Champions League. Three-times an FA Cup winner with us, Mesut won the league title at previous club Real Madrid, and the German cup while at Werder Bremen.

19 SANTI CAZORLA

A star performer for the Gunners ever since his arrival from Malaga in 2012, Santi missed most of last season with injury, making just 11 appearances and scoring twice. A naturally gifted, skilful midfielder who likes to dictate play from the centre of the pitch, Santi's main qualities are his technique and superb vision. He has represented Spain on more than 70 occasions, winning the European Championship in 2008 and 2012.

22 JEFF REINE-ADELAIDE

Exciting attacking midfielder Jeff was regularly involved in the domestic cup competitions last season, making six appearances in all. Since arriving as a 17 year old in summer 2015 though, most of Jeff's football has come at youth level – he often lines up in wide attacking positions, or in the number ten role, but can also play in central midfield. A skilful, tricky, forward-thinking player, Jeff has represented France from under-16 to under-19 levels.

GRANIT XHAKA 29

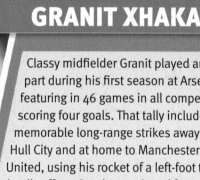

Classy midfielder Granit played an integral part during his first season at Arsenal, featuring in 46 games in all competitions, scoring four goals. That tally included memorable long-range strikes away at Hull City and at home to Manchester United, using his rocket of a left-foot to deadly effect. Granit was signed from German side Borussia Monchengladbach, whom he captained from the age of 22, in the summer of 2016. The Switzerland international is strong in the tackle, a fine passer, and has a fierce will to win.

30 AINSLEY MAITLAND-NILES

Versatile midfielder Ainsley was promoted to the first-team squad last summer after progressing through the youth ranks. He has been at the club from the age of nine, making his first-team debut in the Champions League in 2014, aged just 17. Capable of playing in central midfield, central defence, right back and right wing, Ainsley had a successful loan to Ipswich Town in the Championship during 2015/16 and he helped England win the Under-20 World Cup in the summer of 2017.

34 FRANCIS COQUELIN

A combative and energetic presence in the centre of midfield, Francis is now in his 10th season at the club, having spent much of his early Gunners career out on loan. Following the last of those loans – at Charlton in 2014 – he forced his way into the starting lineup, and has caught the eye ever since. A defence-minded midfielder who breaks up the play well, he was part of our FA Youth Cup winning side in 2009, and played a part in both the 2015 and 2017 successful FA Cup campaigns.

MOHAMED ELNENY 35

All-round midfielder Mohamed had another successful season at the club, impressing with his all-action displays in the middle of the pitch. Adept at anchoring the midfield and surging forward when needed, the Egypt international covers plenty of ground with his tireless running. A winter 2016 signing from Swiss side Basel – for whom he won three successive league titles – Mohamed won our Goal of the Season competition in 2015/16 for his strike away to Barcelona in the Champions League.

Player	Born	Joined Arsenal	Previous Clubs	Arsenal Debut
Jeff Reine-Adelaide	Champigny-sur-Marne, France, Jan 17, 1998	from RC Lens on July 1, 2015	RC Lens	v Sunderland (h) FA Cup, Jan 9, 2016
Granit Xhaka	Basel, Switzerland, Sept 27, 1992	from Borussia Monchengladbach on May 25, 2016	Basel, Borussia Monchengladbach	v Liverpool (h) League, Aug 14, 2016
Ainsley Maitland-Niles	Goodmayes, Aug 29, 1997	as a scholar in summer 2013	Ipswich Town (loan)	v Galatasaray (a) Champions League, Dec 9, 2014
Francis Coquelin	Laval, France, May 13, 1991	from Laval on July 22, 2008	Laval, Lorient (loan), Freiberg (loan), Charlton Athletic (loan)	v Sheff United (h) League Cup, Sept 23, 2008
Mohamed Elneny	El-Mahalla El-Kubra, Egypt, July 11, 1992	from Basel on Jan 14, 2016	El Mokawloon, Basel	v Burnley (h) FA Cup, Jan 30, 2016

FORWARDS

7 ALEXIS SANCHEZ

One of the world's star forwards, Alexis had another incredible season for the Gunners, scoring 30 goals and adding 17 assists. That tally included the opening goal in the 2017 FA Cup final, and an unforgettable hat-trick at West Ham. Often playing as a more traditional centre forward last term, his performances earned him the Arsenal Player of the Season award. Chile's all-time record goalscorer, Alexis is an all-action energetic forward who can also play on the left and won La Liga at previous club Barcelona.

OLIVIER GIROUD 12

Now in his sixth season at Arsenal, Olivier has been a consistent goalscorer throughout his time at the club. He added 16 more goals last season, the pick of which was the amazing 'scorpion' kick finish against Crystal Palace. A physical presence up front who is dangerous in the air, the France international set up the winning goal in the 2017 FA Cup final, the third time he has lifted the trophy. He began this season just two away from a century of Arsenal goals.

Player	Born	Joined Arsenal	Previous Clubs	Arsenal Debut
Alexis Sanchez	Tocopilla, Chile, Dec 19, 1988	from Barcelona on July 10, 2014	Cobreloa, Colo Colo, River Plate, Udinese, Barcelona	v Man City (n) Community Shield, Aug 10, 2014
Olivier Giroud	Chambery, France, Sept 30, 1986	from Montpellier on June 26, 2012	Grenoble, Istres (loan), Tours, Montpellier	v Sunderland (h) League, Aug 18, 2012
Theo Walcott	Middlesex, Mar 16, 1989	from Southampton on Jan 20, 2006	Southampton	v Aston Villa (h) League, Aug 19, 2006
Alex Iwobi	Lagos, Nigeria, May 3, 1996	as a scholar in summer 2012		v Sheff Wed (a) League Cup, Oct 27, 2015
Danny Welbeck	Manchester, Nov 26, 1990	from Manchester United on Sept 2, 2014	Man Utd, Preston NE (loan), Sunderland (loan)	v Man City (h) League, Sept 13, 2014

14 THEO WALCOTT

Long-serving forward Theo has scored more goals and played more games than anyone else in the squad. The pacey right-sided attacker joined the exclusive 100 Club last term, becoming the 18th player in Arsenal history to reach triple figures for the Gunners. The only player to appear in every season at Emirates Stadium, Theo joined us from Southampton aged 16, and is England's youngest ever senior international as well as the youngest player to score a hat-trick for the country.

ALEX IWOBI 17

Now an established member of the first-team squad, Alex progressed through the youth ranks at Arsenal, after joining at the age of seven. He played 38 times in all competitions last term, chipping in with four goals. A skillful, tricky forward who is comfortable playing anywhere just behind the strikers, the youngster burst onto the scene towards the end of 2015/16. The nephew of former Nigeria great Jay-Jay Okocha, Alex is now a full international in his own right, winning Africa Young Player of the Year for 2016.

23 DANNY WELBECK

Strong and athletic forward Danny ended last season on a high, finishing with four goals from just 10 starts. They included a brace against Southampton in the FA Cup on his return from a lengthy injury lay-off. A product of the Manchester United academy, Danny won the Premier League title with his former club, before joining the Gunners on transfer deadline day in summer 2014. Effective either out wide or as the central striker, Danny has more than 30 caps for England.

47

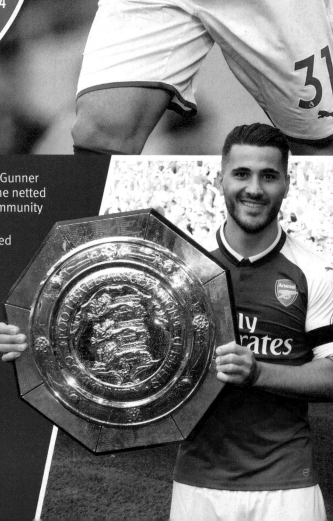

NEW SIGNINGS

SEAD KOLASINAC

Squad number: 31
Position: Defender

Born: Karlsruhe, Germany, June 20, 1993
Joined Arsenal: from FC Schalke 04 on June 6, 2017
Previous club: FC Schalke 04
Bosnia & Herzegovina caps: 18

Combative left-sided defender Sead became the first Gunner to score on his first-team debut for eight years when he netted the all-important equaliser against Chelsea in the Community Shield.

A physically imposing, muscular defender, Sead arrived as a free signing from Schalke in Germany, shortly after being named in the Bundesliga Team of the Season.

Comfortable as a wing back, in central defence or even in defensive midfield, Sead was born and raised in Germany, but represents Bosnia and Herzegovina at international level – the country of his parents. He played at the 2014 World Cup in Brazil, his country's first ever appearance at the finals.

He had spent his whole career at Schalke before switching to north London in the summer, and looks set to become an instant fans' favourite.

ALEXANDRE LACAZETTE

Squad number: 9
Position: Forward

Born: Lyon, France,
May 28, 1991

Joined Arsenal: from Lyon
on July 5, 2017

Previous club: Lyon

France caps:
11 (1 goal)

Prolific striker Alexandre made the perfect start to his Gunners career, netting just 94 seconds into his Premier League debut in the 4-3 win over Leicester City. The French striker became the club's all-time record signing when he joined in July 2017, and soon set about showcasing his natural goalscoring instincts in pre-season.

The forward arrived in north London as one of the hottest properties in French football, scoring 91 goals over the previous four seasons for Lyon, including 28 in just 30 league games during 2016/17, and 37 in all competitions.

Overall he scored 100 times in 203 Ligue 1 matches during his seven seasons with his hometown club.

A natural finisher from an early age, the striker was handed his senior debut as a teenager in 2010, and in 2014/15 he was named Player of the Year, also taking the division's top goalscorer prize with 27 goals from 33 games.

A cool penalty taker, Alexandre was part of the France Under-19 squad – alongside Francis Coquelin – that won the Under-19 European Championship in 2010. France beat Spain 2-1 in the final, with Alexandre scoring the winner. He then made his senior debut for France in 2013.

These three Arsenal youngsters were all selected for the pre-season tour to China and Australia, and all of them impressed despite it being their first taste of first-team football. Find out more about the talented trio working their way through the youth system at Arsenal.

Eddie Nketiah
Position: Striker
Date of birth: May 30, 1999

Eddie has already proved to be something of a goal machine during his short Arsenal career to date. A natural-born finisher, the Londoner has an exceptional scoring ratio, and he doesn't turn 19 until the end of the season. He scored 24 goals from 34 appearances in all competitions at youth level during 2016/17, to add to the 24 goals he scored the previous season. Last term's tally included hat-tricks against Manchester City Under-18s and Leicester City Under-23s and he also grabbed his first competitive goal at Emirates Stadium, when he netted against Manchester United Under-23s. His main weapons are his pace, movement and deadly eye for goal, but he also uses his physical strength to great effect. An England youth international, Eddie joined the Gunners in 2013 after being released from the Chelsea academy.

Reiss Nelson

Position: Attacking midfield/number 10
Date of birth: December 10, 1999

London-born Reiss has developed rapidly through the youth setup at Arsenal, and now regularly trains alongside the first-team squad. A hugely gifted teenager, who can play in any of the attacking positions, but usually favours the number 10 role, Reiss scored 11 times last season, including six for the Under-23s. The pick of the bunch was an audacious finish at home to Chelsea, demonstrating his huge self-belief with a lovely backheeled flick. Long-regarded as one of the most promising players on Arsenal's books, Reiss joined the Gunners aged just eight, and has consistently played above his age group since then. Blessed with wonderful technique and bags of natural ability, Reiss represents England at youth level, and starred at the UEFA Under-17 European Championships in 2016.

He made his first-team debut as a late sub in the Community Shield win over Chelsea.

Joe Willock

Position: Midfielder
Date of birth: August 20, 1999

Creative midfielder Joe has made huge strides over the past year or so, breaking his way into the Under-23 team last season, then being picked for the summer tour to Australia and China.

The younger brother of former Gunner Chris, who joined Benfica last summer, Joe played alongside Chris, and against eldest brother Matt, at Emirates Stadium last season. It was an Under-23 fixture against Manchester United that ended 2-2 – Joe's first appearance at that level. In pre-season he impressed with his fearless nature and tireless work rate. He is able to play in central midfield or further forward. His excellent summer was capped when he was named on the bench for the Community Shield win over Chelsea at Wembley in August 2017. Joe has been at Arsenal from the age of eight, steadily progressing through the Hale End Academy, and signed his first pro contract last season.

51

Do you follow our players on social media? Here's a taste of what they have been posting on Instagram...

@theowalcott Time for some beach football
June 9, 2017

@petrcech Thank you for this award last night – Czech Player of the Year
March 21, 2017

@dannywelbeck Fear = myth.. Views from the 6 #nohands
June 16, 2017

@aaronramsey More moments to treasure
May 22, 2017

@nachomonreal_ Relaxing before meeting up with the national team #Getaria
June 1, 2017

@rholding95 The Arsenal Foundation #nighttoinspire
May 18, 2017

@m10_official Well deserved home win. What luck we could make a young lad happy tonight. #YaGunnersYa #Charlie #Gooner #AFCvSAFC @arsenal
May 16, 2017

@p_mertesacker Nice to welcome our new Academy players to @Arsenal! Good luck boys!
May 26, 2017

@alexis_officia1 Enjoy Gunners, this is for you
May 27, 2017

@hectorbellerin Riding through London, it's all red
May 29, 2017

@jackwilshere The new Mrs Wilshere. On Saturday I married the woman of my dreams! Thank you to everyone who came and made the day so special
June 19, 2017

@granitxhaka She said YES. A golden Ball is a miracle, a golden wife is a paradise! Mr & Mrs Xhaka
June 22, 2017

MIDFIELD MAESTROS

All of these players patrolled the middle of the park for the Gunners, how many can you find?

Arteta	Edu	Jensen	Schwarz
Cazorla	Elneny	Parlour	Song
Coquelin	Fabregas	Petit	Vieira
Denilson	Flamini	Platt	Wilshere
Diaby	Gilberto	Ramsey	Xhaka

V	K	N	N	A	Z	R	A	W	H	C	S	T	R	Q
X	W	C	K	F	U	N	E	S	N	E	J	J	A	Q
R	H	A	C	O	Q	U	E	L	I	N	K	R	M	L
H	H	P	L	D	T	J	D	C	X	P	T	X	S	I
X	T	R	Y	Q	F	Q	S	E	P	T	B	K	E	N
H	A	V	L	M	N	J	A	A	N	V	V	M	Y	I
P	Y	E	M	W	N	S	T	G	G	I	H	Q	N	M
V	D	X	D	N	O	A	E	D	E	E	L	K	M	A
U	Y	N	E	N	L	E	T	I	R	P	R	S	M	L
Z	K	J	G	R	A	J	R	A	E	L	L	B	O	F
X	F	C	O	M	N	R	A	B	H	L	L	A	A	N
K	R	Z	L	G	L	K	I	Y	S	K	D	K	T	F
C	A	N	Z	B	N	W	M	E	L	K	D	M	R	T
C	O	T	R	E	B	L	I	G	I	N	Y	R	H	D
N	M	X	M	P	E	T	I	T	W	V	M	Q	J	L

Words can go horizontally, vertically and diagonally in all eight directions.

Solutions on page 61.

THEO JOINS THE 100 CLUB

With his goal against Sutton United in the FA Cup last season, Theo Walcott gained membership of a very exclusive club. The strike was his 100th for the Gunners, making him the 18th player in Arsenal history to reach the landmark, and only the fourth under Arsène Wenger.

Theo's century of goals came at a rate of one every 3.7 games – the achievement is even more impressive when you consider he has spent much of his Gunners career playing on the wing.

His very first strike was against Chelsea in the League Cup final at the Millennium Stadium on February 25, 2007, when he was just 17.

He has scored in each of the past 11 seasons since then – here's a breakdown of his first 100 goals for the club...

Theo's Century

By competition	
Premier League	63
Champions League	17
FA Cup	11
League Cup	9

By venue	
Home	50
Away	47
Neutral	3

How scored	
Right foot	80
Left foot	15
Header	3
Other	2

When scored	
1-15 minutes	18
16-30 minutes	9
31-45 minutes	19
46-60 minutes	14
61-75 minutes	20
76-90 minutes	19
Extra-time	1

Season by season	TOTAL
2006/07	1
2007/08	7
2008/09	6
2009/10	4
2010/11	13
2011/12	11
2012/13	21
2013/14	6
2014/15	7
2015/16	9
2016/17	15

The 100 Club	Dates at Arsenal	Goals	Games
Thierry Henry	1999-2012	228	377
Ian Wright	1991-1998	185	288
Cliff Bastin	1929-1946	178	396
John Radford	1962-1976	149	481
Jimmy Brain	1923-1931	139	232
Ted Drake	1934-1945	139	184
Doug Lishman	1948-1956	137	244
Robin van Persie	2004-2012	132	278
Joe Hulme	1926-1938	125	374
David Jack	1928-1934	124	208
Dennis Bergkamp	1995-2006	120	423
Reg Lewis	1935-1953	118	176
Alan Smith	1987-1995	115	347
Jack Lambert	1926-1933	109	161
Frank Stapleton	1972-1981	108	300
David Herd	1954-1961	107	180
Theo Walcott	2006-	104	381
Joe Baker	1962-1966	100	156

Get those colouring pens out, why not use Gunnersaurus as a model to design your very own Arsenal kit?

GET COLOURING!

Answer the following question correctly and you could win an Arsenal FC shirt signed by a first team player.

What squad number does Sead Kolasinac wear?
A) 3   B) 13   C) 31

Entry is by email only. Only one entry per contestant. Please enter AFC SHIRT followed by either A, B or C in the subject line of an email. In the body of the email, please include your full name, address, postcode, email address and phone number and send to: frontdesk@grangecommunications.co.uk by Friday, March 30, 2018.

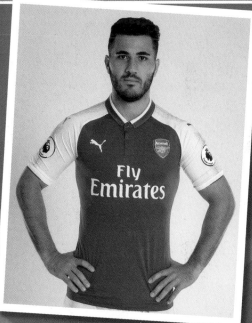

Jonas from Greater Manchester is the lucky winner of last year's shirt competition.

Terms and Conditions

These terms and conditions ("Terms and Conditions") set out the basis on which you can participate in the Arsenal 2017/18 Season Shirt Competition ("Competition"). By entering the Competition, you accept these Terms and Conditions in full. If you do not accept these Terms and Conditions, you should not enter the Competition and you will not be eligible to win the prize. Entry is by email only.

1. COMPETITION PERIOD: The start date for entries is Monday 2nd October 2017 at 16:00 (UK time) ("Start Date"). The closing date for entries is Friday 30th March 2018 at midnight (UK time) ("Closing Date"). Entries received after the Closing Date will not be entered into the Competition. 2. TO ENTER: To enter the Competition, you need to answer the following question: What squad number does Sead Kolasinac wear? A) 3 B) 13 C) 31. Please enter AFC SHIRT followed by either A, B or C in the subject line of an email. In the body of the email, please include your full name, address, postcode, email address and phone number and send to: frontdesk@grangecommunications. co.uk by Friday 30th March 2018. 3. ELIGIBILITY: Entry is open to UK residents only. Only one entry per person is allowed. 4. If entrants are under 18, consent from a parent or guardian must be obtained prior to entry and the parent or guardian must agree to these Terms and Conditions in full. 5. Employees of The Arsenal Football Club Plc (company number 109244) ("Arsenal"), the Promoter or members of their immediate families are not eligible to enter the Competition. 6. Entry is by email only. No purchase is required to enter but you will require email and internet access to enter the Competition. No refund may be claimed for any expenses incurred relating to the use of an email account or internet connection for the purpose of entering the Competition. 7. PRIZE: There will be one prize of an Arsenal 2017/18 season football shirt signed by at least one player for Arsenal's first team (the "Prize"). The Prize is non-transferable and no cash alternative will be offered. 8. SELECTION OF WINNER: The winner will be picked at random from all eligible and correct entries received between the Start Date and the Closing Date. 9. The winner will be contacted using the contact details provided on entry within 72 hours of the Closing Date. If the winner cannot be contacted or does not respond to confirm details for delivery of the Prize within 21 days, an alternative winner will be selected at random from the remaining eligible and correct entries. 10. Unless otherwise notified to the winner, the Prize will be delivered to the winner within 30 days of confirmation of the winner's address for delivery of the Prize. 11. PUBLICITY AND PERSONAL DATA: If the winner is aged 18 or over, the winner agrees to take part in reasonable publicity relating to the Competition and the Promoter and Arsenal may use the winner's name and image and his/her comments relating to the Competition and/or the Prize for future promotional, marketing and publicity purposes in any media worldwide without notice and without any fee being paid. 12. Details of the winner's name and county will be available on request for one month after the Closing Date by writing to the Promoter (including providing a stamped self-addressed envelope) at the address set out below. 13. The Promoter will use entrants' personal details for the purposes of administering the Competition and awarding the Prize. The Promoter may also pass on entrants' details to Arsenal, who may use the details to contact entrants about Arsenal's products and services, in accordance with Arsenal's privacy policy, available at http://www. arsenal.com/privacy-policy. By entering the Competition, you are indicating your agreement to this unless you tell us otherwise. If you do not wish to be contacted or to receive marketing information, you can opt out at any time by emailing AFC STOP to frontdesk@grangecommunications.co.uk. 14. OTHER IMPORTANT INFORMATION: Entries must not be submitted through agents or third parties. No responsibility can be accepted for lost, delayed, incomplete, or for electronic entries or winning notifications that are not received or delivered (for any reason including as a consequence of communication or network failures). Any such entries will be deemed void. 15. The Promoter reserves the right to withdraw or amend the Competition or these Terms and Conditions if circumstances outside its reasonable control make this unavoidable. 16. Entries must be strictly in accordance with these Terms and Conditions. Any entry not in strict accordance with these Terms and Conditions will be deemed to be invalid and the Prize will not be awarded in respect of such entry. The Promoter reserves the right to verify the eligibility of any entrant and to exclude any entries which it believes to be invalid or in breach of these Terms and Conditions. 17. The Promoter's decision is final in all matters relating to the Competition (including the Prize) and no correspondence will be entered into. 18. Except in respect of death or personal injury resulting from any negligence of Arsenal, to the maximum extent permitted by law, neither Arsenal nor any of its officers, employees or agents shall be responsible for (whether in tort, contract or otherwise): i) any loss, damage or injury to you and/or any third party or to any property belonging to you or any third party in connection with the Competition and/or the Prize (including the winner's receipt or use of the same), resulting from any cause whatsoever; or ii) any loss of profit, loss of use, loss of opportunity or any indirect, economic or consequential losses whatsoever and howsoever caused. 19. GOVERNING LAW AND JURISDICTION: The Competition, and any dispute or claim arising out of or in connection with it, shall be governed by and construed in accordance with English law. You irrevocably agree that the courts of England and Wales shall have exclusive jurisdiction to settle any dispute or claim that arises out of or in connection with the Competition. 20. SPIRIT OF THE COMPETITION: If you attempt to compromise the integrity or proper operation of the Competition by cheating or committing fraud in any way, the Promoter and Arsenal each reserve the right to render your entry invalid, seek damages from you and ban you from participating in any of their future competitions. 21. CONTACT: If you have any questions about the Competition, please contact the Promoter. 22. PROMOTER: The Promoter of the Competition is Grange Communications Ltd, 22 Great King Street, Edinburgh EH3 6QH ("Promoter") on behalf of Arsenal.

Can you match the kit to the season?
We've done the first one for you.

1994/95

2002/03

2005/06

2006/07

2011/12

2012/13

2015/16

2016/17

58

Solutions on page 61.

Can you identify the following players, just by looking at their tattoos? The clues are there!

1
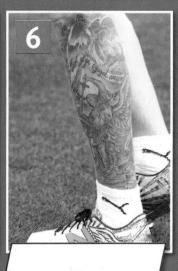

2

3

4

5
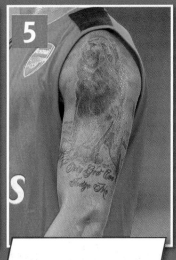

6

7
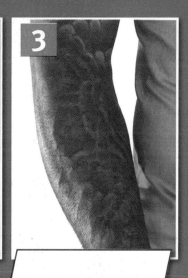

8

9

Solutions on page 61.

Join as a Junior Gunner

Junior Gunners is the youth membership scheme for fans aged 0-16. As a JG member you get to have loads of fun with the club you love; ranging from events for your whole family to fun competitions on the @Gunnersaurus and @JuniorGunners twitter accounts.

JGs get access to a range of benefits, including:

* Discounted match tickets.
* Exclusive events, such as trips to London Colney and Family Fun Days.
* Fun competitions, with prizes such as signed items and match tickets.
* Chances to be a matchday mascot and part of the ball squad.
* Your very own Junior Gunners App!
* 10 per cent off Arsenal Soccer Schools Courses.
* A FREE stadium tour voucher*.
* A cool membership pack*.

There are three tiers of JG Membership: Welcome to our World 0-3; Team JGs 4-11 and Young Guns 12-16. Each tier enjoy their own events and competitions. To find out more and to join today, head to alwaysaheadofthegame.com/junior

*Full Membership Only

JUNIOR GUNNERS

QUIZ ANSWERS

How well do you think you did on the quizzes?
Check all your answers below.

Page 28 – Spot The Difference

Page 29 – Cup Kings

1. Olivier Giroud
2. Seven
3. Yellow and blue
4. Manchester United
5. 1930
6. David Seaman
7. True
8. Three
9. 2-1 to Hull
10. A replay
11. Ray Parlour and Freddie Ljungberg
12. 1997/98
13. 4-0

Page 33 – Who's Older

1. Mesut Ozil
2. Per Mertesacker
3. Aaron Ramsey
4. Hector Bellerin
5. Mohamed Elneny
6. Theo Walcott
7. Sol Campbell
8. Ray Parlour
9. Ian Wright
10. Robert Pires

Page 54 – Midfield Maestros

V	K	N	N	A	Z	R	A	W	H	C	S	T	R	Q
X	W	C	K	F	U	N	E	S	N	E	J	J	A	Q
R	H	A	C	O	Q	U	E	L	I	N	K	R	M	L
H	H	P	L	D	T	J	D	C	X	P	T	X	S	I
X	T	R	Y	Q	F	Q	S	E	P	T	B	K	E	N
H	A	V	L	M	N	J	A	A	N	V	V	M	Y	I
P	Y	E	M	W	N	S	T	G	G	I	H	Q	N	M
V	D	X	D	N	O	A	E	D	E	E	L	K	M	A
U	Y	N	E	N	L	E	T	I	R	P	R	S	M	L
Z	K	J	G	R	A	J	R	A	E	L	L	B	O	F
X	F	C	O	M	N	R	A	B	H	L	L	A	A	N
K	R	Z	L	G	L	K	I	Y	S	K	D	K	T	F
C	A	N	Z	B	N	W	M	E	L	K	D	M	R	T
C	O	T	R	E	B	L	I	G	I	N	Y	R	H	D
N	M	X	M	P	E	T	I	T	W	V	M	Q	J	L

Page 58 – Kitted Out

4	○――――――○	1994/95
5	○――○	2002/03
6	○――――○	2005/06
8	○――――○	2006/07
1	○――――――○	2011/12
2	○―――――――○	2012/13
7	○――○	2015/16
3	○――――――○	2016/17

Page 58 – Guess the Tattoo

1. Hector Bellerin	2. Santi Cazorla	3. Alexandre Lacazette
4. Olivier Giroud	5. Mesut Ozil	6. Aaron Ramsey
7. Theo Walcott	8. Jack Wilshere	9. Granit Xhaka

WHERE'S GUNNERSAURUS?